D1809483

The TDD Companion

By Scott L. Bain

Introduction from the author:

I was by no means an early adopter of Test-Driven Development. When it was first suggested (by Ward Cunningham) that developers should write tests for their own code I felt that this was not a good idea at all.

I was concerned that this would overload developers with too much work to do, that the time it takes to write tests would take away from the main job of development. I was concerned that someone who wrote the code would write a test that was insufficiently challenging, too "friendly" to it. I also wondered what the testers were going to do once the developers were writing the tests. Do we not need their expertise and experience?

I have completely changed my views on this. I am not only in favor of TDD, but in fact I have become a staunch advocate for it. What changed my mind was TDD itself. Once I tried it (somewhat against my will) it almost immediately began to prove itself to me. Over the years that I've been teaching it I've seen the same thing happen to my students. TDD moves from a burden being imposed on us to a powerful tool that helps us to do our job better, to gain confidence about our code. It increases the value we bring in our work. It helps us to work faster while decreasing risk

I also had the good fortune to meet Amir Kolsky. Over the years of having Amir as a colleague, I have learned much of what is in this book, especially regarding the distinctions that make TDD sustainable.

This book is meant to be a lightweight companion to the TDD practitioner. Each entry is a page long at most. These pages are loosely organized, except where specific pages relate to each other. The idea is that you can pick it up, open it anywhere, and gain a useful insight without having to spend hours poring over it.

This book is not a primer on TDD; plenty of those already exist (see the bibliography on pg. 61). It is intended to help you engage in TDD more effectively. I hope you will find it valuable.

Table of Contents

Many people, when asked to define "Test-Driven Development" will say something like "That's where the developers write tests before they write the code." That is "test-first", and it is a part of TDD, but just because you're writing tests before code does not mean you are necessarily doing TDD.

Test-first is an analysis process; it helps us determine what is clear, what is unclear or missing, and ferrets out misunderstandings. Unit tests are unforgiving, they don't let you get away with anything.

But Test-Driven Development also creates better design. Bad design is hard to test, and so moving tests into a primary position reveals the pain of a bad design very early, before much commitment has been made to it.

Also, TDD requires a set of skills that includes refactoring, dependency injection, mocking, and many others. To do TDD effectively, developers must possess all of these skills and know how to use them in the process.

Write your tests first; but learn how to **listen** to what they tell you about your product design, and how to use them to drive quality into the system. Much of the rest of this book intended to help you learn how to listen to your tests in this way.

TDD Causes a Shift in Thinking

Project Managers and Product Owners are sometimes dubious about the development team doing TDD. They are concerned that the team will slow down because they've been burdened with additional work, and that developers might "game" the system with bogus tests to satisfy the process. Also, it seems like a nonsensical idea to write a test for something before that thing exists.

All of these concerns are addressed by the observation that, despite its name, TDD is not really a testing activity. The "tests" that are written in TDD are actually the *specification* of the system. The effects of this shift in thinking are profound.

First, it is not at all odd or strange to think of the specification preceding development. Specification has always come first.

Second, it is not a new task, but an old task done in a new way, and a better way because the specification can be executed against the code.

Third, developers would never "game the specification," because they value it highly; the spec tells them what to do and leads them to success. Everyone wants to succeed.

Finally, TDD does not replace traditional testing. So, the testers are not removed from the process, they are simply given more time to do their job.

People often object to the notion of developers writing tests because, they claim, developers are already fully engaged in their jobs and should not be given additional work to do. If they are burdened with testing as well as development, this will negatively impact their velocity.

In fact, the reality is just the opposite. TDD is a single activity that pays you back for your effort in multiple ways. TDD tests pay you back:

- When you are writing them. They help you to understand the problem you are attempting to solve, they reveal gaps in your knowledge, and lead you to useful questions.
- When they fail. They inform you of a defect and, if written well, specifically where that defect is.
- When they pass. When you are enhancing or refactoring the system, tests passing confirms that you are making only the changes you intend to make.
- When you read them later. Tests capture knowledge that might otherwise be lost.

In TDD we create a *specification of the system*, using unit tests to do so. Creating a specification is not new work; we were going to do this anyway. TDD is about leveraging the specification activity to provide all the value listed here, and more.

When TDD was first suggested, there were many who were dubious about the wisdom of having developers write tests of their own code. Among the objections raised was that developers will slow down if you burden them with new tasks, namely writing the tests as well as the code.

This seems logical. Give someone more to do, and they will take longer to do it. But the truth is that TDD actually increases velocity once the team gets over the initial learning curve. How can this be? This is true for three reasons.

First, **TDD makes developers proactive**. They tend to be less hesitant when everything they do is being constantly confirmed or corrected.

Second, **TDD helps developers to avoid writing unnecessary code**. Developers will sometimes "chrome" the system when they are not certain about exactly what the code needs to do. Defining behavior in tests first helps them to avoid this.

Third, **TDD is really about creating a specification**, which we were going to do anyway. It's not really new work, but a new way to do existing work. It is a way that can be confirmed at any time in the future to be correct.

TDD speeds up the team.

TDD is a process that provides constant confirmation to the development team.

Writing the tests up-front confirms that there is sufficient understanding of requirements so that they can be expressed in the rigorous form of a unit test. Alternately, it reveals that this understanding has gaps and reveals questions that need to be answered.

The quality of the test mirrors the quality of the system, and so if "good" tests (as defined in this book) can be written, this is confirmation of a good design.

Running the test initially and watching it fail confirms that the test is legitimate. One potential mistake in TDD is writing a test that has no way to fail. Seeing it fail confirms that this kind of error has not been made.

Making the test pass confirms that the work done on the system produces the correct behavior. And seeing all the pre-existing tests *continue* to pass confirms that only the intended change was made.

This constant confirmation breeds a kind of confidence that is traditionally rare in software development. Such confidence is attractive to developers: once they experience it, they never want to go back! It also leads to aggressiveness.

A typical question those adopting TDD ask is: How much testing is enough? Or, put another way, does everything really need to be tested? How do you decide what to test and what not to test?

It's an interesting question, but I prefer to address it this way: everything *will* be tested. The real question is, by whom? Will it be you, or someone else?

Defects detected quickly, by you, are addressed in a much cheaper way than those detected and reported by your customers. Those are expensive in terms of the time it takes to find them and in terms of the reputation of your products and your organization overall.

Also, you have to consider the possibility that your customers will encounter a defect and never tell you. That means that one of these is probably true:

- They are suffering with it.
- They don't trust you to fix it.
- You have created features that nobody uses.

These are all bad things. TDD identifies useful behavior and ensures it is correctly implemented.

Some organizations who have adopted TDD as their development strategy have assumed that they no longer need SAT/QA testers, since the developers are now writing tests. **This is a mistake.**

First, developers do not write the same kinds of tests that testers do. Developers write the tests they need to drive correct behavior into the system. They do not cover all of the edge and corner cases, because their focus is on creating useful behavior.

Second, skill in testing is not the same as skill in development. Experienced testers will approach the system from a different point of view than developers will, and this has tremendous value.

Third, there are many different kinds of tests that the developers won't do at all such as usability testing, stress testing, and various forms of exploratory testing. Much of this kind of testing cannot be meaningfully conducted until after the system is fully functional.

Developers doing TDD will significantly contribute to the QA effort by supplying many of the low-level unit tests that testers would otherwise have to write, and this means that the testers are free to do more of the sophisticated testing that often gets cut due to time constraints. But we still need the testers' experience and skill to do this properly.

In many large organizations there is a kind of wall between development and testing. This can create negative attitudes on both sides.

Developers see testers either as a source of no information ("It works? Yeah, we knew that") or bad news ("There are bugs to find and fix, ugh"). Testers are adversaries to overcome before developers can be said to have succeeded.

Testers see developers as a source of hard work, and code that must be wrestled with. Often testing lags hopelessly behind development and because of this, testers see developers as a source of a never-ending avalanche of work.

When these organization adopt TDD, this unhealthy adversarial relationship tends to fade away. Developers who write tests are far more understanding of what drives testers, and they personally experience the value of tests. Testers see developers as a source of the low-level unit tests that they can inherit, and thus no longer have to write. This frees them up to do the more interesting testing that often gets cut due to time constraints. TDD also drives the defect rate down dramatically, so testers find themselves able to keep up. Everybody wins. TDD makes developers and testers into valued colleagues, and so improves the health of the culture. This contributes to improved products and less waste.

A test reacts to *everything* currently in scope that it does *not* control.

Ideally, that should be only one thing. Everything else in scope, therefore, must be controlled by the test or it may react to the wrong thing and give misleading results.

For example, if a production entity uses a service call as part of its implementation, and the service being called is *not* what the test is testing, then that call must be controlled by the test because it is in scope. If the test fails, we want to know that it is not a failure of the service but rather of the code that calls it: the code currently under test.

This is a major reason to use a mock[1] object. Anything which is in scope, but which we are not currently testing, should be replaced by some form of test double, which in TDD is typically called a "mock object".

Knowing how to create mocks, how to get them inserted into the system when the tests are running, and how to use them to confirm the specific intent of the test is a major aspect of being an effective TDD developer.

---

[1]

http://www.netobjectives.net/patternrepository/index.php?title=The MockObjectPattern

"Getting to green" is not the goal of TDD. Automated tests pass by default -- a test that contains no code at all will register as green. By itself this is meaningless.

No, in TDD it is **observing a red (failing) test turn green** that proves everything.

The <u>red test</u> proves the validity of the test (that it can fail, that is has meaning). Tests need a reason to fail, and this reason reflects the desired behavior of the system. Tests that cannot fail are actually worse than no tests, because they mislead the developers and promote confidence based on false confirmations.

The <u>green test</u> proves the production code has been made accurate to the meaning of the test. The code is written to pass the test, and so we know that it will forever be covered by the test going forward.

The <u>transition</u> from red to green proves that the test and the production code are connected to each other. This is because we make failing test pass not by changing the test, but by changing the code.

TDD creates, therefore, semantically meaningful test coverage. Nothing else can ensure this.

Part of the TDD process consists of writing failing tests before the code that will eventually make them pass. When tests are written before production code, this has several beneficial effects. They comes from the fact that these tests have the same orientation toward the code that client code will have in the future. Tests are, essentially, the first clients of any behaviors they drive into the system. Here are some examples of what this means.

- Interfaces will be driven from the clients' needs. This is compatible with the Gang of Four[2] recommendation to "design to interfaces."
- Tests will identify any vulnerabilities that clients will experience beforehand. For example, if the test needs to use magic numbers in order to execute, this tells you that clients will have to do the same thing.
- Redundancies in tests that cannot be factored out is a warning that future clients will contain redundancies.

These are just examples. TDD causes us to develop behavior from "the outside-in." This enhances reusability and limits coupling.

---

[2] "Design Patterns: Elements of Reusable Object-Oriented Software, Gamma, Helm, Johnson, Vlissides

TDD, when conducted as a *specifying* activity, is an aspect of Behavior-Driven Development (BDD)[3]. Behavior is what we specify and is what we "drive" into the system using tests. Therefore, when structuring the tests in TDD we can be guided by the language of BDD: **Given, When, Then.**

Given the system is in a known condition, ***when*** an event occurs, ***then*** the system should be in the correct new condition.

Any behavior can be specified in this way, and the description is understandable by everyone in the organization because we all grow up learning about the concept of cause and effect.

Where TDD differs, however is that we make this actionable and thus executable. We change the terms accordingly. Some like to use Arrange, Act, Assert, other prefer Setup, Trigger, Verify, etc… but in any case, we turn the nouns of BDD into the verbs of TDD; nothing is "given," we make it so. We don't wait for "when," we do it. We know the "then" because we observe it.

When writing tests in TDD, we take pains to make sure these three different anatomical parts of the test are as distinct and clear as possible to future readers.

---

[3] https://en.wikipedia.org/wiki/Behavior-driven_development

Ideally in TDD, no more than one test is ever failing at any given point in time. This test represents the work that is about to be done but hasn't yet. Also, this test should not spend a long time in the red. We want the suite to get back to "all green" as quickly as possible.

Here are some reasons for this:

- To return to passing tests frequently, developers are encouraged to work in small steps. This reduces the likelihood of errors and also reduces the waste that task-switching can produce.
- Whenever the suite is all green, the code can be committed to version control. The longer you wait to do this the more likely you will be required to perform merge tasks, which have no real business value.
- It is the nature of daily business that we sometimes get interrupted. If we are forced to break away abruptly, then when we return later it may be hard to re-gather the context of the work we were doing. If tests had been all-green only a few minutes before the interruption, then "falling back" does not mean a lot of work will be lost.

Children are encouraged to eat in small bites and to chew their food thoroughly, so that they will not choke, rush, or overeat. Doing TDD in a small feedback loop follows this same principle.

You cannot meaningfully test that which you do not adequately understand. The time to find that out is before you start development. TDD helps us to determine what we do not know. Sometimes, it tells us what our stakeholders don't realize they also don't know.

Imagine you are developing the software for a casino's poker slot machine (loosely based on a real case). Part of the behavior needed is to shuffle the "cards", mixing them up into a new order. That would be the stated requirement. If we try to write a test about this, we realize that this is not nearly detailed enough. What is meant by a "new order"? How new? How will we know when the shuffling is adequate? Are there any regulatory requirements about this? Industry standards? Not being casino experts, the developers probably don't know and would ask the customer. The customer might realize that they aren't clear themselves.

Testing something requires far more rigor than most people apply to their businesses, and that means the development team that does TDD not only finds good questions to ask but can also help the customer to more fully understand their own business domain. At times, this leads them to realize even more business value than they knew they wanted.

Magic Buttons

Here is a bit of a thought experiment[4]: Imagine there are two magic buttons in front of you. You know, without any doubt that if you press button A then your code will suddenly have 90% code coverage. If you push button B, it will have 80% code coverage.

But there is another difference.

If you press A, only 10% of your code will be uncovered by tests. But you will have *no idea* where that 10% in the system.

If you press B, 20% of your code will be uncovered by tests. In this case, however, you will know *exactly* where that uncovered code is.

Which would you press? If your answer is B, which most people choose, it tells you about your true attitude towards risk. We eliminate all risks we can but once we have done that it is more important to know where the remaining risks are than to eliminate a few more of them blindly.

What coverage really means, and how we achieve it in TDD, is all about this. We'll consider that next.

---

[4] This was suggested by a colleague, Eran Pe'er.

It's not unusual these days for development organizations to adopt a code coverage requirement. This is usually expressed as a percentage: at least X% of all code developed must be covered by tests.

Measurement tools are used as a process gate, where the team must achieve this minimum coverage level before code can be checked in. **This is pointless and may be dangerously misleading.** Code coverage tools can only measure how many lines of code are *executed* by tests, but not what the test *do* with the results of that execution.

A test can call all the public methods of a class, assert that 1+1=2, and coverage will appear to have been achieved. Why would a developer do this? To get past the process gate.

In TDD we don't measure code coverage for this purpose. We don't need to. All code is written to satisfy failing tests. These tests were written to express a requirement and provide needed guidance to developers and is therefore meaningful. Developers write these tests to help them make their work and careers successful, not to satisfy an externally imposed regulation.

Don't trust semantic-free code coverage measurements. Trust the TDD process and its connection to self-interest.

TDD and Code Coverage Tools

In the previous page, we established that code coverage tools do not provide useful project metrics, in and of themselves. In TDD, we don't use code coverage tools for this purpose because we don't need to. If all production code is written to satisfy prewritten, failing tests, then by definition, all code is covered.

Still, we do have automated tools that can measure coverage. Are they useful to a TDD practitioner? Yes, they are. Here are three things they are useful for.

- To ensure that all developers are following this process. We watch code coverage to make sure it never goes down. If it does, we need to find out how and why the process wasn't followed.
- Sometimes, developers put temporary code into the system to help them investigate, understand, or track something. This code should be removed once the investigation is done. If code coverage slips, there may be "dead code" that was left in the system.
- Sometimes, we determine that a test is no longer needed. When we remove such tests, we examine code coverage before and after their removal. This confirms that we were right to delete them.

Strong tools are great, but we don't want them to take over our process. We want to use them to *support* it.

It is important that the system behaviors we create as developers are both accurate and precise. These are not the same thing because one can be:

Accurate, but not precise: "Pi is a little over three."

Precise, but not accurate: "Pi is 5.393858303895."

They are related, however, in that the level of precision required tells us how far to go in determining accuracy.

An example: the system is required to trigger a process "immediately after midnight". "Immediately" can only be determined to be *accurate* if we know the level of precision in the requirement. Is it one second after? One tenth of a second? One hundredth? By "after" do we really mean the behavior should be triggered *at* midnight, since computers do not behave instantaneously? Should we use the clock speed of the machine to determine what "immediately" means?

One big advantage of TDD is that automated tests require concrete information. They do not allow us to accept requirements without truly understanding both the accurate and precise version of them, because we can't write the test code correctly without this information. If developers see the unit tests as specifications (and given that we know not to "make things up") then when questions like these arise we are forced to get more detail.

Software is quite often implemented in the context of reusable frameworks and other pre-existing, valuable entities. For example, if code is written that is required to send data over a TCP-IP connection in, say, C#, the tendency is for the developer to use the built-in Socket class that is part of .Net. Why would a developer create their own such entity? It makes sense to reuse what is well tested and proven over time to be effective.

The problem this causes for TDD is that in order to test drive the code being developed, we'd need to specify that the information sent over the socket was well-formed, that it confirms to the requirements. We could create a loop-back on the network to "catch" the information being sent, but this is a fair amount of effort and will tend to produce a test that is too slow to run frequently.

The better solution is to wrap the framework entity in an adapter[5]. This would be mostly just a pass-through, and so it would be simple to create. But it creates an inflection point. Such an adapter can be mocked for testing, and thus eliminate the need to control the real socket.

Avoid direct coupling to reusable components.

---

[5]

http://www.netobjectives.net/patternrepository/index.php?title=The AdapterPattern

19

In TDD we want to run the tests frequently. When we do so, it shortens the pulse of our work, increasing velocity. Also, when a test unexpectedly fails, we know that it must be something we just did that produced this effect. It becomes very easy to find the error. This means that we must be *able* to run tests frequently which in turn means that tests:

1. Must run fast
2. Must be able to run at any moment

The first point is the topic of the next page. The second requires that the tests can be run without any specific pre-conditions on the system. No test should require a specific time of day, a specific location in the world, a specific condition of the database, UI, or other system element, or anything that would mean the developers cannot run the tests whenever they desire, almost as a reflex.

Tests should feel like they *cost nothing* to run. In truth, nothing costs nothing, but the cost of running tests should be so low that developers don't hesitate to run them frequently.

Tests, in other words, should be repeatable and independent. To achieve this, developers must be well trained in good test design, the separation of concerns, and strong techniques like mocking, shunting, endo-testing, dependency injection, etc...

As an agile process, TDD needs to be responsive and flexible, and part of this is the ability to keep the feedback loop between tests and production very short.

To run tests frequently without excessive cost requires that tests must execute quickly. Anything that the developer can do that makes a given test even a little bit faster, so long as it does not reduce the quality of the test, is worth doing. Here are some things that keep tests fast:

- Use constant values rather than variable ones. If you establish a value in a test instrument, and the test will not need to change this value, make it a constant.
- Don't allocate memory you don't need. Example: Sometimes we need to build an instance just to confirm the build, but we won't need the instance for anything later. Just build it, don't assign a reference to it.
- Stay away from slow dependencies. The Database, network, file system, etc... will all slow your tests down immensely. Mock out these connections.
- Avoid loops, conditionals and other complex code structures in your tests. They should execute from top to bottom. This makes them faster, but also easier to read as specifications.

These little changes will be important once the suite has a large number of tests.

Defects can either be prevented or detected.

Let's say you write a method in Java that takes, as its parameter, one of the nine players on a baseball team.

If you decide to make that parameter an integer (1 is the pitcher, 2 is the catcher, and so forth), then the code will still compile if a number greater than 9, or less than 1, is passed into the method. You will have to take some action in the code if that happens: correct the data, throw an exception, something along those lines. This code would be written to "detect" the defect and would be driven from a failing test in TDD.

On the other hand, you would not have to allow for the possibility that someone will pass a non-integer, like 1.5, into the method, because the compiler (in languages like Java) will not allow this. Anything the compiler, linker, IDE, etc. will not allow is considered a "prevented" defect.

In TDD, we do not write tests for prevented defects. But any defect that cannot be prevented must have a test or the test suite is incomplete.

Therefore, any defect that makes it into production is not considered a defect at all in TDD. It is a missing test.

Figuring out the test you missed is job one.

In TDD, there are always more potential scenarios to test, other than the "happy path" of desirable behavior. We need a way to decide how far to go.

This is often a question of risk assessment. Having a framework for thinking about risk can be useful. Consider the concept that risk that has at least two dimensions: **Likelihood** and **severity**. Crossing these produces a four-quadrant matrix. Most risks exist somewhere within these dimensions

Very likely and highly severe. *Example from life: Being in a car accident.* They happen all the time and can kill people. These are worth taking action on, like installing seat belts and airbags.

Unlikely and trivial. *Example from life: My neighbor's mail being delivered to my house.* This almost never happens, but if it does, I just take it next door.

Unlikely and highly severe. *Example from life: Being struck by lightning.* Most of us will never experience this, but it would be bad if it happened. You might install lightning rods on your home, but that's a judgement call.

Very likely and trivial. *Example from life: Stubbing your toe.* This happens to everyone on a fairly regular basis, but it's only annoying. I don't bother to wear steel-toed shoes around the house.

Testing vs. Testability

We should consider testing, which is an activity, versus testability, which is a quality of design.

If we start with the word "test" itself, we note that it is both a noun and a verb. I can say, "I have a test for that behavior," or I can "test a behavior." As a noun, it is an artifact that can express the nature of a desired behavior (if the test is written first) and it can capture that knowledge for the future. As a verb it can drive that behavior into the code, and then be used to subsequently verify its correctness later.

"Testability", on the other hand, is a quality of the system being tested. What kinds of tests *can* you write about it? What kinds of test do you *have to* write about it? What will tests tell you when they fail? How much effort is required to create these tests?

The fact is, bad design is hard to test. We see this with a lot of legacy code: it has no tests, or the tests are very slow and cumbersome. When we try to test something and find the effort to be extremely difficult, this can be called "pain", and pain is a diagnostic tool. That's why pain exists.

This pain can be revealed whether you actually write the tests or not. It is certain to be revealed if you do. The earlier, of course, the better.

TDD and Coupling

In TDD, the test suite can serve as a tool for quantitatively analyzing the qualities present (or absent) in the production code.

One example: A test will need to access the production entity that it is testing, obviously. However, sometimes a test needs to access another entity or entities as well, even though they are not currently under test. We can refer to these collectively as a "fixture" for the test.

Some tests have no fixture. The entity in question can be tested entirely on its own. Business rules are often like this. Some tests have a small fixture of an entity or two. Some have large fixtures of many entities.

Fixtures are a measurement of coupling. Look at a given test suite, total the size of the fixtures overall, and divide by the number of tests. This is a measurement of the coupling in the system being tested. Is it large? There is a lot of coupling.

This is not to say that all coupling is bad. But a large average should raise a concern and indicates that coupling is an issue worth looking into.

This is just one example. Tests not only provides a mechanism for analyzing the problem, but also the quality of the solution, and this analysis can be far more concrete than we usually experience. Numbers are numbers.

Tests in TDD can reveal the extent that the **Single Responsibility Principle**[6] has been adhered to.

The Single Responsibility Principle states that every class in a design should have a single responsibility. The reason that tests will reveal when this principle has been violated has to do with the number of tests needed for that class' behavior.

For example, let's say a class is responsible for connection to an HTTP service, but also has to validate that the data returned adheres to a domain-specific language. Tests would have to be written that ensured the connection was made properly, and other tests that the DSL was accurately applied. But because both behaviors exist in the same class, tests would *also* have to be written to ensure there were no side-effects between these behaviors: that the code that validates the DSL did not "step on" any state needed for the connection, and vice-versa.

Systems that violate the SRP often see test packages that are far larger than the production code packages. This is because of these additional "protective" tests that are needed.

---

[6] https://en.wikipedia.org/wiki/Single_responsibility_principle

TDD and Encapsulation

The type and nature of the tests that you write in TDD helps you to understand how strongly your system is encapsulated.

Everything the system *must* do, and yet might not, needs a test. Here, "must do" comes from your stakeholders' requirements and is therefore connected to business value. The more your tests are about these issues, the clearer your specification will be.

Everything the system must *not* do, and yet might, needs a test. Here, "might" means that the unwanted behavior is possible, that it cannot not prevented in some way. Anything that the compiler, linker, etc. will catch and report is prevented and does not require a test. If such tests were written, it would be impossible for them to fail.

Weak encapsulation allows for more of these negative behaviors to make it into the executable, where tests are needed to raise the alarm. So, the more negative tests you need, the less encapsulation you have achieved.

Of course, part of this depends on the technology you use. Languages like Java and C# have constructs like private class members and enforced type-checking, and so more negatives can be stopped by the compiler. JavaScript, and the like, have less of these restrictions and so more protective tests will be required.

The Open-Closed Principle[7] states, "Software entities (such as classes, modules, and functions) should be open for extension, but closed for modification."

This means that a "good" design will allow for a new behavior to be added to a system without having to change the existing code, or at least to minimize those changes.

Of course, one cannot perfectly achieve such a thing, but trying to get as close as possible leads to systems that are far more resilient and extensible in the face of new requirements. TDD relates to this in the following way:

When enhancing an existing system in TDD, we *always* start by writing a new (failing) test. The idea is then to do the work needed to make that test pass. The question is, in doing this, did we break the older tests? If so, then we have discovered a lack of "open-closed-ness," and we should investigate. If not, then we can confirm that our system does indeed follow this principle, at least in the area of concern.

No one can follow their principles perfectly, but when we do not follow them we need to know about it, because this represents an identified risk.

---

[7] https://en.wikipedia.org/wiki/Open–closed_principle

TDD and the Separation of Concerns

One aspect of strong design is that separation is created between the various concerns of the system. This adds clarity, promotes re-use, and improves cohesion.

It can be difficult to know, however, if one has separated things sufficiently, or perhaps has overdone it. This is one area where TDD can help. Example: An object with asynchronous behavior has, at minimum, two categories of concerns.

1. The main behavior the object is responsible for delivering to the system.
2. The thread-safety of that behavior, that it is re-entrant or that it properly prevents race conditions, etc.

Normally a developer would simply use the provided mutex that the framework supplies to ensure the behavior was thread-safe, and this would be part of the implementation of the main behavior. However, when trying to test that safety, it is quite difficult to simulate threading problems to ensure that the right actions are taken. This leads to a separation of these concerns, using a Design Pattern called the Synchronization Proxy[8]. This makes the testing much easier, but also shows us: **TDD is also Test-Driven *Design*.**

---

[8] Details: http://www.sustainabletdd.com/2014/10/tdd-and-asychronous-behavior-part-1.html

In TDD, we seek to create granular, unique tests, tests that fail for a single reason only. To achieve this, when testing an entity that has dependencies, we create mocks of those dependencies. A mock[9] can be simply a replacement that the test controls.

As with every part of TDD, mocking can tell you things about the design of your system.

What might be obvious is this: when a large number of mocks are needed, this indicates a large number of dependencies that must be dealt with when testing a given entity. A large number of dependencies indicates a lot of coupling, which can be problematic when maintaining the system.

However, mocking also can tell us something else. Mocks, ideally, are kept very simple. We want them to have no way to cause the test to fail and thus mislead us.

If we find that we cannot create a mock simply, this means that the dependency it replaces may be too complex. It may lack cohesion or do too much, and the need for a complex mock is reflecting this.

---

[9] https://portal.netobjectives.com/pages/learning/webinars-and-podcasts/mock-objects-mock-turtles/

"Refactoring" refers to the discipline of improving the design of existing code without changing its behavior[10]. It is usually thought of as a way to deal with old legacy code that is functional but poorly designed and thus hard to work with. Since TDD focuses on driving new behavior from tests, how would refactoring play a role in a TDD team? In three ways:

New code, generated to make a failing test pass, can be immediately refactored under the protection of the test. This keeps code from accumulating debt over time.

Test code, like all code, should adhere to the rules of good design: tests, after all, have to be maintained too. The skills that developers learn to refactor older code can also be used to clean up tests when they are passing but have quality deficits.

Changing (enhancing or debugging) legacy code can be dangerous because it usually lacks adequate tests. In TDD, the first step is to refactor the code proximate to the proposed change *just enough* that a high-quality test can be added. Then, code can be enhanced under the protection of that test. This is test-driven change and is part of TDD.

---

[10] "Refactoring: Improving the Design of Existing Code", Martin Fowler

Most organizations have some type of reporting mechanism allowing customers to alert them to defects they have encountered. Typically, a "trouble ticket" or similar artifact is generated, and someone is assigned the debugging task. They must first locate/replicate the defect and then fix the errant code. TDD views this very differently.

In TDD, a "defect" is code that *causes a test to fail* after development was thought to have been completed. If buggy code makes it into production and is released to customers, this is not a defect. It is a missing test.

The critical task at this point is to determine what test was missed. We actually do not want the production code to be fixed at this stage, because once we find what we believe to be the missing test, we want to be able to:

- Write the test.
- Run it and watch it fail.
- Make it pass by changing the production code (only).

Because the test is made to pass solely by changing the production code, we can be sure we have indeed written the correct test. This is a more valuable way to deal with a defect because once the test is in place, the defect can never return as we do not release code which has failing tests. It is **permanent** debugging.

"Good" Tests in TDD

As consultants, we are often asked to review the work of others. One of the things we review is the quality of the design of some part of the system. Is it cohesive, decoupled, non-redundant, encapsulated, open-closed, and so forth? Often the developers understand and agree that these qualities are important, but they are not certain they have achieved them adequately.

I often start like this, "I don't know. Can you write a *good* test for it?" I can ask this even before I look at their work because I know that bad designs are notoriously hard to test. It's a great way to start an evaluation. Of course, the trick to this is understanding what is meant by a "good" test.

In TDD, we focus on three specific aspects of tests, each of which I will write about separately in upcoming pages:

1. The test must fail reliably for the reason intended.
2. The test must never fail for any other reason.
3. There must be no other test that fails for this reason.

These three statements describe an ideal, and of course in the real world they are not always perfectly achievable. But understanding "good" in this way helps to determine the design qualities mentioned above because, lacking them, writing "good" tests becomes increasing difficult.

TDD requires an expenditure of developer effort. All such effort is an investment, and thus should yield a return. TDD returns value in many ways, but here I will focus on one way in particular:

Tests prove their worth when they fail.

When a test fails, this is the point when we say "wow, we're glad we wrote that test" because otherwise there would be a defect in the system that was undetected. But we can also ask how *much* value a test's failure provides, and the answer is that the value is relative to the quality of the information it provides in that failure.

When a test fails for the reason it was intended to, this means several things:

1. That intention was clearly understood when the test was written.
2. That intention is clearly documented because of *the way* the test was written.
3. The exact nature and location of the defect is made extremely clear.

Most developers will tell you that the tricky thing about debugging is not fixing the bug, but rather finding what and where it is in the code. Good tests find bugs.

When a test fails for a reason other than intended, then upon investigating the cause of that failure the natural assumption will be that it *is* failing for the reason intended. Thus, the failure will mislead the team into investigating the wrong problem.

Anything that wastes developer time is to be avoided resolutely. Developer time is a highly crucial resource in modern development in that a) you need it to get anything done, and b) you can't make more of it than you have. There are only so many hours in the day, and only so much time, focus, and energy a given person can devote to a task. Wasting this resource is like burning money in the street.

Furthermore, if a test fails for a reason other than you intend, then you obviously have created a test that has more than one failure mode which, if you understand TDD well, would not have been your intention. Investigating how this happened is a real opportunity to improve your process once you identify the problem and focus on it.

Finally, if the errant thing that is making your test fail *also* has its own test (which, in TDD it absolutely should), then you're also violating the third aspect of "good" tests. I will write about that next.

When organizations adopt TDD as their development paradigm, early results can be quite good once the teams get over the initial learning curve. Code quality goes up, defect rate goes down, and the team gains confidence which allows them to be aggressive in pursuing business value.

But there is a negative trend that can emerge as the test suite grows in size over time.

Generally speaking, TDD is an Agile process and so new requirements flow into the team on a regular pulse, through push or pull. A new requirement in TDD always means a new, failing test. Then, work is done to make this new test pass. However, sometimes this causes older tests to fail. These tests must be maintained, and this work feels wasteful as it adds no new value. Over time, more and more older tests must be maintained as new requirements are prioritized and, eventually, the process seemingly becomes *unsustainable*.

This is avoidable and is in fact a subject that high-quality TDD training should focus on.

When two tests fail for a single reason this indicates that this problem has begun and must be addressed before it gets worse. Understanding that his is not acceptable is the first step to correcting it.

TDD and Design Patterns

Design patterns in software came from the work of the Gang of Four in the mid-1990's. Similarly, TDD was first promoted around the same time in history as part of eXtreme Programming. Some have suggested that these two points of view stand in opposition to each other, saying Design patterns are about up-front design, while TDD is about emerging design through the test-first process.

In truth, TDD and design patterns are highly synergistic. Understanding each of them contributes to your understanding of the other.

First, design patterns represent a focus on specific qualities in design. These very same qualities lead to greater testability, especially when creating the kinds of tests TDD requires. But also, each pattern can include in its collection of best practices the ideal way to test a given pattern, and again "ideal" in the sense that the tests empower TDD.

And finally, TDD includes refactoring the code as we go, and often the refactoring of the code leads to well-understood design patterns. If the team understands this, it massively aids in collaboration.

TDD and design patterns work together because they value the same things.

Because TDD is "test" driven development, people tend to think of TDD as "writing tests first." In fact, TDD is not a testing activity *per se*. It is the creation of an executable specification prior to the creation of each system element. Unit tests are a very useful by-product of this process.

Because of this point of view, TDD dictates that different tests be written, or written differently than the QA point of view would lead us to do. There are points of overlap, but there are distinct differences, and this means that those new to TDD often miss certain important tests.

Typically, these missing "executable specification" tests will include:

1. Public constants
2. Only one side of a boundary is specified
3. Critical internal workflows
4. Exceptions thrown by the system

In the next few pages, I will provide details on what these things are and why it is important they be included in the TDD suite of tests.

TDD is different from QA in many respects. Part of this involves the tests we choose to write. A case in point is the specification of public constants.

Example. When businesses buy assets, they can write-off (amortize) the value of those assets over time, as a taxation issue. The government will dictate how quickly a given asset can be amortized, which is called the "term" for amortization. If the term for writing-off an automobile was given to be five years by the IRS, developers would likely create a constant, **AUTO_TERM** or something similar, and assign it the value of 5. This constant would be used in any code that needed to perform a related calculation, rather than hard coding a literal "5" everywhere. It's a best practice.

QA would find nothing to test here, it's just a value. TDD on the other hand dictates that *no code* can be written unless a failing test is written first. That test would indicate that the constant exists, what its name is, where it is placed, and the current value. This puts the value into the test suite, where it is preserved for the future as part of a complete specification.

This also means that we can test-drive the change to this value when the government changes the law. This preserves our process as well as ensuring the accuracy of the change.

Often a given behavior will change due to a certain condition: sometimes the system will behave one way, sometimes another. We call this kind of behavioral change a "boundary" and it should be specified as such in TDD.

For example, let's say there is a business rule that dictates how a passed-in value should be handled. If the value is greater than 100, we decrease it by 10%; a kind of quantity discount.

Those new to TDD might simply specify that a value of 101 should be decreased by the system to 89.1. But this is not enough. Boundaries have two sides, because two behaviors are implied by this rule: to apply the discount, and not to. Therefore, we need two tests. One would show the discount being applied, and the other would show the value was unchanged.

But we also need to show the degree of change in the value needed to trigger the behavior. Is it 1 over 100 (as our test says)? Is it 0.01 (pennies, if this is money)? Is it smaller? Larger? A test should specify this "epsilon" as well.

Creating the test suite as a "detailed executable specification" helps us to ensure that all important business information is captured.

In the previous page I wrote about the necessity in TDD of specifying both sides of a behavioral boundary, and its epsilon. This is important because we want a complete, detailed record of the critical business rules and other values in the system. But there is another reason that this is important. It has to do with the notion of "a specification."

Why do we want a specification, as developers? Simply put, it is to help us to write the correct code. The *best* specification, therefore, would *ensure* we write the correct code. It says, "If you make a mistake, I'll tell you right away."

If, as I mentioned in the previous example, we wrote a test that said, "A value of 101 will be reduced to 89.1." that test would pass if the code always applied the 10% discount, no matter what the value is. That would be the wrong code, but the test would pass. It would not alert us to our error.

If the boundary is fully specified, however, we will *have to* put a conditional into the code, and if the epsilon is specified, then the conditional will *have to* be implemented with the right level of precision.

That's what good specifications do and only TDD makes them executable/automated. They become enormously valuable to developers as they guide us to success.

The term "workflow" in this sense is meant to indicate the way two system elements interact when performing a task. Often these interactions themselves are not exposed outside the system, and so only their resulting behavior should be tested. This is as true in TDD as it is in traditional testing.

Most workflows are implementation details that developers should be able to change so long as the right behavior is still achieved. If the developers have a better idea, or technology improves, these changes should not break tests.

However, there are some workflows that *are* part of the specification and must not be altered. For these we must have a test.

Consider a system that has a layer which provides access to a database. In this case it is critical that all accesses to the database go through this layer (where, perhaps, business rules or regulatory requirements are enforced). We realize that it would be possible for a developer to "go around" this layer and directly access the database (perhaps for performance) without realizing that this violates a requirement.

TDD should have this critical workflow specified in a test which would now fail, alerting the developer to the error immediately: You can't go around the access layer.

Specifying a workflow in TDD means writing a test that says, "When entity A is called upon to accomplish a task, it must interact with entity B is the following way." This is done when the interaction in question is part of a required workflow, and not simply an implementation decision that should be changeable.

The best way to accomplish this is to create a mock of entity B. Such a mock would "log" how it is used by entity A at test time, and then allow the test to examine the log and compare it to what should have happened. There are many ways to accomplish this[11].

However, care must be taken to engage in this form of testing *only* when the workflow is part of the customer-defined specification. Doing it in other cases will create excessive coupling between the tests and the system under test. This hamstrings any refactoring efforts that follow.

Powerful techniques are helpful, but never stop thinking about how you are using them.

---

[11]

http://www.netobjectives.net/patternrepository/index.php?title=The MockObjectPattern

Exceptions in software represent a mechanism for raising an alarm when something goes wrong. They are used when there is a potential problem that cannot be detected by the compiler, linker, or other automated aspect of the development process, and thus may potentially make it into the released product.

When an exception is declared in the code, it is basically a way of saying, "We hope this never happens, but if it does at least we'll be made aware of it." Getting the exception is bad news, but the problem that caused it is made visible so we can deal with it. Not getting the exception is good news. Everything is fine.

In TDD, however, this is logically reversed.

If the decision is made that an exception *should* be thrown under a given situation and if, in a test of that situation, it is indeed thrown then this is *good* news. The system is behaving as intended. It is when the exception should have been thrown but was *not* that we have a problem to deal with. Not getting the exception is the bad news.

Throwing exceptions is a behavior of the system. Like all behavior it must be part of the specification and in TDD, this means it must be driven by a test that initially fails. Exceptions, in other words, are no exception. 😊

TDD and System Architecture

When first adopting TDD, developers can run into some roadblocks that seem to indicate that TDD is a difficult process. In truth, some of these problems actually indicate faults in the system architecture.

For example, developers will struggle to write unit tests of behavior that is embedded in a user interface, or in stored procedures in a database. Allowing a test to "push a button" in a UI involves the user of complex tools and tends to slow down the test execution. The same is true if the test has to spin up the database.

Another example is testing application logic when it is peppered throughout with framework calls or calls to web-services or other external dependencies that are difficult or impossible to control during the test run.

This is a big subject, but the bottom line is this: TDD encourages a clean separation of business logic from other layers of the system. This is a good idea anyway; it means that the same application can be deployed using different UI's (web vs mobile, for example), or using different technologies for persistence. It promotes the re-usability of business rules without redundancy.

Bad design is hard to test. So is a weak architecture. TDD helps you to see this early.

Developers often remark that the tests may contain the same algorithms that the production code does. This feels like redundancy. Example: A system that converts Fahrenheit to Celsius. The code would contain something like this:

```
return (F - 32) * 5/9;
```

The test might assertion this:

```
assertEquals((F - 32) * 5/9, result);
```

This seems like a redundancy, but it is not. It is duplication. Duplication is "the same thing." Redundancy is "things that change together."

The algorithm in the test is included to *specify*. The algorithm in the production code is to *implement*. One could change independently from the other. The clearest way to specify something is not always the most efficient way to implement it. If the developers decided that a better way to implement this behavior was:

```
return (F-32) / 1.8;
```

This would not require the test to change. Specifications always record domain knowledge. Implementations apply this knowledge. If they match this is a coincidence, not a problem.

TDD and Naming: Part 1, Test Names

TDD is not really a testing activity so much as it is about the creation of an executable specification. Because of this we value different things than testers might. Naming of tests, variables, and the use of well-named customized assertions are examples.

Test names are sometimes provided by the tools we use. Many IDE's will allow you to submit a class or an interface to a function that will create an empty set of test methods for you, one per public method it finds. These tools are to be avoided in TDD.

For example, if you had a class that represented a bank account which had a public method `GetValue()`, the suggested test would likely be `TestGetValue()`.

In TDD, we would focus instead on the best way to describe this behaviorally. The fact that the method happens to be "`GetValue()`" is irrelevant; we would want the test to be named something more like:

```
TestRetrievalOfCurrentBalance();
```

...something which would be accurate whatever the specific syntax of the implementation happened to be. This seems trivial at first but becomes much more important when are hundreds of tests someone is trying to read five months from now in order to understand the system.

Tests often establish example values used to compare the behavior of the system with the actual behavior indicated in the requirements. For example, if we had a system behavior that converted Fahrenheit to Celsius, then the test that specified this might have an assertion along these lines:

```
assertEquals(100,
converter.fahrenheitToCelsius(212));
```

However, the use of these values directly in the assertion sidesteps an opportunity to express the meaning of those values in the specification. Why did we choose 212 and 100, specifically? If there is a reason, then we would want to capture that information as well. The creation of temporary variables, sometimes called "instrumented values" creates this opportunity. For example:

```
int boilingPointFahrenheit = 212;

int boilingPointCelsius = 100;

assertEquals(boilingPointCelsius,
converter.fahrenheitToCelsius(boilingPo
intFahrenheit));
```

This makes the test more readable as a specification.

Unit testing frameworks, which are the most common tools used by developers to conduct TDD, come with pre-made assertions that can be used to verify the behaviors being specified. Typically, these include assertions such as:

`areEqual(e, a)` (value comparison)

`areSame(e, a)` (entity comparison)

`isNotNull(x)` (entity creation)

`contains(x, c)` (collection contents)

Developers should not limit themselves to these pre-made assertions. The creation of custom assertions is a best practice. Here are some advantages.

- They yield more expressive tests. The custom assertions are named using behavioral, domain language. For example: `employeeWasAddedToDatabase(e)`.
- The tests can end up shorter and more focused, and therefore easier to read.
- You have more control over the message emitted in the test runner when the test fails.
- They can be used to eliminate redundancies across tests.

Custom assertions are implemented using the canned assertions, and so they are equally reliable.

In TDD, tests take actions such as Setup, Trigger, and Verify. Each of these pieces must successfully execute in order for the specification to be verified as accurate to the current behavior of the system.

If there is an external dependency, the test can become vulnerable to a failure of that entity. For example, If the system requires the use of an object factory in order to get an instance of a class, then the test will have to use that factory in order to get the instance. If the test is not a specification of the factory, but rather is a specification of a behavior in the entity it builds, nevertheless a defect in the factory could cause the test to abnormally end.

A developer might be tempted to put a conditional into the test code:

if the factory fails,
then abort the test,
else conduct the test as normal.

This would be done to prevent the test suite from crashing due to a null pointer exception. A better way to do this is the use of a **guard assertion**. Basically, anything which must be true for a test to continue executing is asserted to be true. In the example, it could be `assertNotNull(x)`.

If false, then the test will stop and fail in an orderly manner rather than crashing.

One controversy in software development is the relative value of strong, static typing (as in compiled languages like Java) vs. dynamic typing (as seen in interpreted languages like JavaScript). No attempt will be made here to engage in this debate, but it is interesting to note the role of TDD in languages that are not statically typed.

For example, in Java, you could design a **Square** class that required a "height" and "width" to be passed in via its constructor. You could define that both height and width must be integers, and if code exists that attempts to create a **Square** by passing in something other than integers the code would fail to compile. No test would be created to guard against this. What might be a run-time error would be caught instead at compile time.

However, in JavaScript, there is no compiler. Code that attempted to create an instance of **Square** by passing in floating point numbers, or strings, or null would execute with perhaps unpredictable results.

TDD can help here for those who prefer dynamic typing. When such a restriction is deemed important extra tests can be added to ensure that critical parameters are of the correct type, moving the detection of potential errors from run-time to test-time.

TDD often uses unit tests to drive behavior into the system. However, sometimes acceptance tests are used to do this. When these are automated, this can give us clues as to how to make our work in TDD more reusable.

Tools like Fit, Specflow, and Cucumber are all designed to parse some non-technical artifact (such as tables, text, and images) and then execute the semantics as tests. These frameworks are designed to look for methods, written by developers, that can be used to trigger behavior which they then verify. These methods are variously named "Step Definitions," "Glue Code," "Binding Methods," etc.

But there is no reason that unit tests cannot utilize such methods to trigger behavior. If these methods will be needed for acceptance test automation, you can reduce the burden on developers by *training them to write their unit tests this way in the first place*. If they do this, then when it comes time to automate acceptance tests, their part in the process is already done.

This is because of something we call "test invariance." No matter how you express the specification of a behavior, that expression should be testable at any level in the system, and with any set of tools, as the expression chosen does not change the meaning of the spec, or the test.

Abstract classes in languages like Java or C# serve two purposes: they create polymorphism in design, and they are a convenient place to put behavior that is common to all derived classes, avoiding redundancy.

But if all behavior in TDD needs to be tested, and if instance behavior implemented in abstract classes cannot be tested (because they cannot be instantiated), then how can we adhere to our process?

Abstract classes have subclasses. An instance of any one of those subclasses will have access to the common behavior implemented in the abstract base class, so the developer could simply pick any one of them and test the common behavior using it. The problem with this is that it couples the test of the common behavior to a specific subclass, which is not preferred.

This is another use for a kind of mock: a subclass is created only for testing. It is part of the test suite, not a public class, and is specifically designed to be convenient for testing. This is also called a "testing adapter" and is a best practice in TDD. Not only does it decouple the test from other implementations, it can be crafted to make it easier to test (adding public methods that call protected ones, for example).

The Value of Refactoring Skills

Refactoring is defined by Martin Fowler as "improving the design of existing code." Refactoring stipulates two things: that behavior does not change, and that the design has been improved. Fowler made this a discipline that developers can collaborate within. He defined a shared way to do it, and names for each refactoring.

In TDD, we support refactoring by ensuring that all code has behavioral tests associated with it, which can then be used to ensure behavior has not, in fact, changed. Refactoring is also part of the TDD process itself.

1. Learning It is used to improve legacy code, which is often functional but expensive to work with due to a weak design.
2. It helps developers to keep production code and test code from decaying over time.
3. It enables just-in-time design where code is refactored immediately proximate to changes being made, in order to make those changes safer and cheaper.

Learning how to refactor efficiently and effectively takes time and effort, often through training and coaching/study sessions. The skills gained through this effort apply to multiple aspects of development.

Learning strong refactoring skills isn't free, but it pays the team back in many ways.

TDD is a powerful way to develop new code. However, most organizations have significant existing code that was not developed this way. This "legacy code" is often difficult to test because it was not designed to be testable in the first place.

In his excellent book, Working Effectively with Legacy Code[12], Michael Feathers outlines techniques for making legacy code more testable. It's is an essential resource for anyone that has significant legacy code. But how do we incorporate these activities into TDD? Organizations can't afford to simply stop and fix all their legacy code.

Focus on occasions when legacy code must be changed. We begin by using Feathers' techniques to get the portion of the code that will need to change under some kind of test. This may not be a "good" test in the TDD sense. But it will reflect the current behavior of the system. It is then changed to reflect the new requirement and allowed to run and fail. The system is then updated to make it pass.

If changes to legacy code are always accomplished this way, then the system will always be continuously improving, and gradually can be brought under the TDD umbrella. This will be incremental, but also very realistic.

---

[12] https://www.amazon.com/Working-Effectively-Legacy-Michael-Feathers/dp/0131177052

Most requirements are statements of desired behavior. But there can be implications behind these requirements concerning behavior that is not desired.

For example, we might test-drive a value object that represents some domain information, and the requirement for it might include that the object must be "immutable". The implication would be that the object has no mutator methods allowing the values contained to be altered.

How can we write a test that specifies that a method does not exist? Test code that tried to access a non-existent method would obviously not compile. You might think "add a set method that throws an exception if called". But throwing an exception was not the requirement.

TDD is about **specification**. Specifications have a two-part rule about this:

1. Specification must be complete. No behavior exists that is not in the specification.
2. Given **#1**, anything *not* in the specification is *not* in the system.

Thus, the lack of a test that specified that there *is* a mutator method means there isn't one. This is assured if we follow the process that says no code is created without a failing test.

At this point in these pages on TDD. I wanted to bring some of this material together and engage with the notion of TDD as a sustainable process. In this page I will introduce the topic, and then cover some issues that pertain to sustainability and/or the seeming lack thereof.

There are those who have concluded that TDD is a great way to start a project and "get it on its feet," but should not be continued past the first few iterations of work. Their argument is that, as the test suite grows in size and complexity, the maintenance burden it places on the team eventually becomes too much of a distraction from the actual work on production code, and TDD has to be abandoned in favor of the traditional code-then-cover approach.

Some have gone so far as to say that "TDD is dead" because of this.

If I believed this, I would not have spent the considerable time and effort I have in writing about it here. And I would not have taught TDD and coached TDD countless times and in countless places around the world.

TDD is not a magic bullet. Nor is anything else. But it *can* and *should* be a sustainable process. The next, final pages will address some of the apparent challenges that arise and what those challenges tell us.

TDD is typically part of an agile process. This means that we embrace change, that new requirements flow into the team's work either on a time-boxed pulse, or through some kind of pull system (like Kanban). In TDD, a new requirement always starts out as a new, failing test or "specification." We write the test to express the requirement before it has been fulfilled.

Then, work is done in the system to make this new test pass. Over time, however, developers begin to experience the syndrome where making the new test pass makes older tests fail. Those tests must be maintained (you cannot leave tests "in the red") which burdens the team. This problem tends to get worse over time.

Some interpret this as being an inherent cost of TDD, but in fact it is an indication of coupling. If one test causes another test to fail, then it would appear the tests are coupled to each other. But testing frameworks are designed to stringently protect against this. What this means is that the effect observed in the tests is actually an indicator of excessive coupling in the system. The tests are coupled to each other through their connection to the production code.

We don't "live with this." We use it as a diagnostic tool to improve the health of the system.

Project managers have to balance resources. Spending them on one thing means not spending them on another. So, when the team adopts TDD, it is understandable that attention is paid to the level of resource needed to sustain it over time.

It's not uncommon for project managers to notice, as the project grows, that the creation of tests and their maintenance seems to be an increasingly large drain on resources. Team leads may note that the suite of tests is actually larger than the production code base, sometimes far, far larger.

When this happens, an examination of the test suite will very often reveal that many of the tests in it are not written to express the specification of desired behavior, but rather to guard against unwanted behavior (bugs). These "protective tests" do not express business value, they indicate a lack of encapsulation in the system. If there was more robust encapsulation, they would not be needed because more bugs would be prevented by the compiler or run-time engine.

This could mean the design is weak or that the technology being used lacks enough enforcement of encapsulation, but in any case, it is a diagnosis of a problem which should be addressed. If it is, the test suite will end up fundamentally smaller and cheaper to maintain.

TDD depends on a strong connection between the automation of the test suite and the system itself. The suite should record the specification that is implemented in the system, and the connection allows this to be confirmed at any point.

The problem is: automated tests pass by default. So, if errors creep into the test code that breaks the connection to the system (the tests are not really doing anything) they would still pass under most circumstances.

As with any code base, the larger the suite becomes the more likely it is that such errors will be creep in. This would seem to indicate a finite size for a test suite before it becomes unreliable. The solution is this: not only must every *behavior* of the system be driven from a test that fails initially, but so must every *change* to the system going forward.

When a behavior must change, in TDD, the test must be changed first and run to observe its failure. This ensures that the test is legitimate (can fail). Then, the change is made to the system. The test is run again and is observed to pass even though the test code was not touched. This ensures that the right change was made and that the tests and the system are still strongly connected.

TDD is a powerful process. But it only works if you follow it.

Bibliography

Essential Test-Driven Development
by Robert C. Myers
Addison-Wesley Professional
ISBN-10: 0134494156
ISBN-13: 978-0134494159

xUnit Test Patterns: Refactoring Test Code
by Gerard Meszaros
Addison-Wesley Professional
ISBN-10: 9780131495050
ISBN-13: 978-0131495050
ASIN: 0131495054

Test-Driven Database Development: Unlocking Agility
by Max Guernsey III
Addison-Wesley Professional
ISBN-10: 032178412X
ISBN-13: 978-0321784124

Test Driven Development: By Example
by Kent Beck
Addison-Wesley Professional
ISBN-10: 9780321146533
ISBN-13: 978-0321146533
ASIN: 0321146530

About the Author

Scott Bain is a 40-plus-year veteran in computer technology, with a background in development, engineering, and design. He has also designed, delivered, and managed training programs for certification and end-user skills, both in traditional classrooms and via distance learning. Scott teaches courses and consults on Agile Analysis and Design Patterns, Advanced Software Design, and Sustainable Test-Driven Development. Scott is a frequent speaker at developer conferences such as JavaOne and SDWest. He is the author of "Emergent Design" which won a Jolt Productivity Award. He is also the author of "The TDD Companion" and is a co-author of "Essential Skills for the Agile Developer".

Since 2000, Scott has worked for Net Objectives: https://www.netobjectives.com

Email: slbain@netobjectives.com
Personal blog: www.slbain.com
TDD blog: www.sustainabletdd.com

Printed in Great Britain
by Amazon

36198392R00040